HEINEMANN
STATE STUDIES

Uniquely
New Jersey

Mark Stewart

Heinemann Library
Chicago, Illinois

Designed by Heinemann Library
Page layout by Wilkinson Design
Printed and bound in the United States by
    Lake Book Manufacturing, Inc.

08 07 06 05 04
10 9 8 7 6 5 4 3 2 1

**Library of Congress
Cataloging-in-Publication Data**

Stewart, Mark, 1960-
  Uniquely New Jersey / Mark Stewart.
       p. cm. -- (State studies)
Summary: Provides an overview of various aspects
of New Jersey that make
it a unique state, including its people, land,
government, culture,
economy, and attractions.
Includes bibliographical references and index.
   ISBN 1-4034-0677-4 (HC library binding) -- ISBN
1-4034-2687-2 (PB)
   1. New Jersey--Juvenile literature. [1. New Jersey.]
I. Title. II.
Series.
   F134.3.S755 2003
   974.9--dc21

2003010353

Acknowledgments

The author and publishers are grateful to the
following for permission to reproduce copyright
material:

Cover photographs by (main) Bob Krist/Corbis;
(row, L-R) Charles Rex Arbogast/AP Wide World
Photo, Joseph Sohm/Visions of America/Corbis,
Lee Snider/Corbis, Hector Emmanuel/Heinemann
Library

Title page (L-R) Hector Emmanuel/Heinemann
Library, Hector Emmanuel/Heinemann Library,
Corbis; contents page, p. 7b, 8t, 9t, 38 E. R.
Degginger/Color Pic, Inc.; p. 6 Joseph Sohm/
Visions of America/Corbis; p. 7t OneMileUp.com;
p. 8b Robert Landau/Corbis; p. 9b Karen Carr;
pp. 11, 24 Daniel Hulshizer/AP Wide World Photo;
p. 12 Mike Derer/AP Wid World Photo; p. 15 Patti
Sapone, Pool/AP Wide World Photo; pp. 16, 19,
33, 36, 37t, 39, 43, 44 Hector Emmanuel/
Heinemann Library; pp. 17, 26t, 41 Michael S.
Yamashita/Corbis; pp. 18, 30 Reuters NewMedia
Inc./Corbis; p. 20t Kelly-Mooney Photography/
Corbis; p. 20b Columbia/The Kobal Collection;
p. 21 Christie's Images/Corbis; p. 22 Rusty
Kennedy/AP Wide World Photo; p. 23 James
Leynse/Corbis SABA; p. 25 Robert Maass/Corbis;
p. 26b Brian Branch Price/AP Wide World Photo;
pp. 27, 29 North Wind Picture Archive; pp. 28t, 31
Corbis; p. 28b www.piratehaven.org; p. 32
Bettmann/Corbis; pp. 34, 37b Bob Krist/Corbis;
p. 40 George Goodwin/Color-Pic, Inc.; p. 42
Maiman Rick/Corbis SYGMA

Photo research by John Klein

Special thanks to expert reader Chad Leinaweaver,
the Director for the Library at The New Jersey
Historical Society, for his help in the preparation
of this book.

Every effort has been made to contact copyright
holders of any material reproduced in this book.
Any omissions will be rectified in subsequent
printings if notice is given to the publisher.

Some words are shown in bold, **like this.**
You can find out what they mean by looking
in the glossary.

Contents

The Garden State 4

New Jersey State Symbols 6

New Jersey State Government 11

New Jersey's Food 16

Art and Culture 18

New Jersey's Sports 21

Business in New Jersey 23

Legends and Lore 27

Attractions and Landmarks 33

New Jersey's Bridges and Structures 40

Map of New Jersey 45

Glossary 46

More Books to Read 47

Index 48

About the Author 48

The Garden State

New Jersey is a unique state. Something that is unique has uncommon or hard-to-find features and characteristics. One thing that makes New Jersey unique is that it is the most **urban** state in the country. Ninety percent of New Jersey's population lives in urban areas. In addition, New Jersey is also the most **densely** populated state, with more people per square mile than any other state.

New Jersey's history also makes it unique. One of the state's nicknames is Cockpit of the Revolution. It refers

Unique Facts About New Jersey

1846—First baseball game played: New York Nine vs. Knickerbockers, Hoboken

1869—First college football game played: Rutgers vs. College of New Jersey (now Princeton), New Brunswick

1877—Phonograph invented: Thomas Edison, Menlo Park

1877—First submarine built and tested on Passaic River: John Holland, Paterson

1879—Incandescent lightbulb invented: Thomas Edison, Menlo Park

1889—First electric sewing machine made: Singer Manufacturing Co., Elizabeth

1889—First motion picture produced: Thomas Edison, West Orange

1896—First professional basketball game played: Trenton vs. Brooklyn YMCA, Trenton

1933—Nation's first drive-in movie theater opened: Camden

1952—Solid-body electric guitar developed: Les Paul, Mahwah

Things to See in New Jersey

to the **American Revolution** (1775–1783). More than 100 battles were fought in New Jersey between the Continental Army and British troops. A turning point in the war occurred when General George Washington led his army across the Delaware River and surprised the British at Trenton in 1777.

Two of the world's greatest inventors also worked in New Jersey for part of their careers. Samuel F. B. Morse (1791–1872) invented the first successful U.S. electric telegraph in Morristown. During the 1870s, Thomas Edison (1847–1931) invented the incandescent lightbulb and the phonograph in Menlo Park, and he produced the first motion picture in West Orange in 1889. Read on to find out more interesting and unique things about New Jersey.

New Jersey State Symbols

NEW JERSEY STATE FLAG

The state flag, which bears the state seal, is blue and buff. Buff is a gray-yellow hue that is identical to the color of **piping** on the uniforms of New Jersey's soldiers during the **American Revolution.** Legend has it that George Washington (1732–1799) himself selected this color. New Jersey's official motto—Liberty and Prosperity—also appears on the flag.

The New Jersey state flag was adopted in 1896.

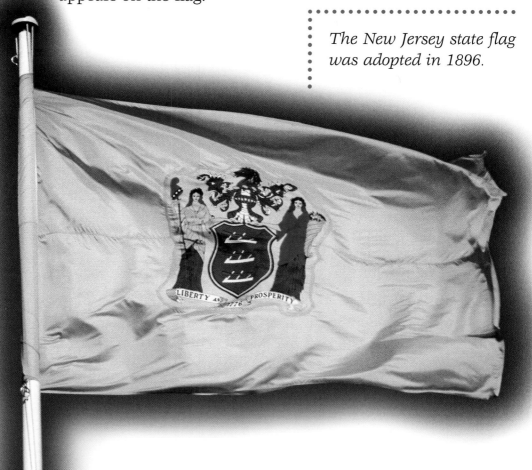

NEW JERSEY STATE SEAL

New Jersey's state seal was designed by Pierre Eugene du Simitiere and presented in 1777 to the New Jersey **legislature.** The state seal has a shield with three plows. The plows represent the richness of New Jersey's soil and its hardworking people. The horse's head at the top honors an animal that is still a key part of the state's **culture** and **economy.** One of the two figures on the seal is Ceres, the Roman goddess of grain. She is holding a **cornucopia** overflowing with crops, symbolizing New Jersey's agricultural success. The second figure is Liberty. She represents the state's freedom. Between the two figures, a forward-facing helmet symbolizes New Jersey's independence.

The year 1776 at the bottom is the year of New Jersey's independence.

STATE BIRD: EASTERN GOLDFINCH

In 1935, the New Jersey legislature adopted the eastern goldfinch as New Jersey's state bird. This yellow-and-black bird darts between bushes and trees and is common in New Jersey.

The eastern goldfinch measures about five inches long.

The meadow violet ranges in color from deep violet to white.

STATE FLOWER: COMMON MEADOW VIOLET

First introduced by the New Jersey **legislature** in 1913, the common meadow violet was finally adopted as the state flower in 1971. It grows in any of New Jersey's 50-plus state parks. In fact, the violet grows all over the state and does best in the cool, shadowy fringes of open fields.

STATE TREES: RED OAK AND DOGWOOD

In the fall, the colorful leaves of the state tree, the red oak, transform the landscape. The red oak was adopted in 1950. In the spring, the state's **memorial** tree, the dogwood, delights with its bright white flowers and attracts bird and animal life. The dogwood was adopted in 1951.

STATE SHELL: KNOBBLED WHELK

In 1995, New Jersey designated the knobbled whelk as the

The height of a dogwood ranges anywhere from 10 to 40 feet.

official state shell. A walk along the Jersey Shore might turn up this pear-shaped shell.

STATE NICKNAME: THE GARDEN STATE

On August 24, 1876, at the Centennial Exposition in Philadelphia, a man named Abraham Browning gave a speech on New Jersey Day. Borrowing from an earlier description of New Jersey by Ben Franklin, he described his home state as a huge barrel, open at both ends, from which New York and Philadelphia got their produce. He used the term Garden State, and the name became hugely popular.

The knobbled whelk shell is pear-shaped and is about three inches long.

STATE DINOSAUR: HADROSAUR

The hadrosaur, which was named New Jersey's official dinosaur in 1991, has been in a Philadelphia museum since its discovery in the 1800s! In the summer of 1858, a man named William Parker Foulke was vacationing in Haddonfield, New Jersey, when he heard that twenty years earlier, workers had found large bones in a **marl** pit. Foulke hired a crew of diggers and eventually found the bones of an animal larger than an elephant with features of both a lizard and a bird. Foulke had discovered the world's first nearly complete skeleton of a dinosaur. Today, the historic site is celebrated with a stone marker and a small park.

The typical hadrosaur measured nearly 50 feet in length and had rows of hundreds of teeth.

New Jersey State Quarter

The New Jersey state quarter's design is based on a painting by Emmanuel Leutze entitled *Washington Crossing the Delaware* (1851). The painting is currently hanging in the Metropolitan Museum of Art, in New York City.

It's (un)Official!

New Jersey has no state song. However, in 1972, a song entitled "I'm From New Jersey" by Red Mascara was proposed as the official song. It passed both **legislative** houses, but governor William Cahill never signed it into law.

I'm From New Jersey

I know of a state that's a perfect playland with white sandy beaches by the sea;

With fun-filled mountains, lakes, and parks, and folks with hospitality;

With historic towns where battles were fought, and presidents have made their home;

It's called New Jersey, and I toast and tout it wherever I may roam. 'Cause . . .

Chorus

I'm from New Jersey and I'm proud about it, I love the Garden State.

I'm from New Jersey and I want to shout it, I think it's simply great.

All of the other states throughout the nation may mean a lot to some;

But I wouldn't want another, Jersey is like no other, I'm glad that's where I'm from.

Chorus

If you want glamour, try Atlantic City or Wildwood by the sea;

Then there is Trenton, Princeton, and Fort Monmouth, they all made history.

Each little town has got that certain something, from High Point to Cape May;

And some place like Mantoloking, Phillipsburg, or Hoboken will steal your heart away.

New Jersey State Government

New Jersey's **capital** is Trenton. This is where New Jersey's elected officials help to run the state.

NEW JERSEY'S CAPITOL

New Jersey's **capitol** was built in 1792. A man named John Doane designed the state capitol on a 3.75-acre site that the state originally bought for around $400. The original building stood 2.5 stories tall, with a huge center hall leading to seven different wings.

New Jersey governor Christie Whitman holds a rededication ceremony for the capitol dome on June 24, 1999.

An 1885 fire led to the building of a new **rotunda** and dome. In the three decades that followed, New Jersey further improved the state house and enlarged it.

More recently, from 1996 to 1999, the dome was covered with 48,000 pieces of gold leaf. Children raised the money used to purchase the gold leaf. New Jersey rededicated the dome to its schoolchildren when it was done. All told, the new dome cost about $9 million.

STATE GOVERNMENT

New Jersey's first state government was set up before the state house was ever built. It met for the first time in 1776 and wrote New Jersey's first state **constitution.** The most recent New Jersey state constitution was adopted in 1947. It, like the ones before it, is similar to the U.S. Constitution. The legislative branch makes the laws. The executive branch, which includes the governor, runs the state's day-to-day affairs. The judicial branch applies the state's laws to the people.

New Jersey Governor James McGreevey (center podium) *talks to the New Jersey legislature about his budget on March 26, 2002.*

LEGISLATIVE BRANCH

New Jersey's **legislature** is made up of two houses: the senate and the general assembly. The legislature traces its first meeting back to the summer of 1776. During the **American Revolution,** British forces were poised to occupy the state and turn it into a transportation route between New York City and Philadelphia. Work began on New

Executive Branch

Governor
(four-year term)

Carries out the laws
of the state

Legislative Branch

New Jersey General Assembly

40 State Senators (varied term)	80 Assembly Members (two-year term)

Makes laws

Judicial Branch

Supreme Court

Superior Court

Appeals Court
Tax Court
Municipal Courts

Interprets the laws

Jersey's constitution in June. The legislature met on August 27, 1776, and approved this constitution. It was followed by two later drafts, in 1844 and 1947.

Today, the people of New Jersey elect **legislators** from 40 different districts, or areas. Each district chooses one state senator and two members for the **general assembly.** This means that the state senate has 40 senators and the general assembly has 80 members. Members of the legislature make the state's laws.

The length of time that senators serve varies in New Jersey. A population **census** is taken in the United States every ten years. New Jersey senators are elected to a two-year **term** in the election after each census. Then, the next two terms are each for four years. Members of the general assembly, on the other hand, always serve for two years. The New Jersey legislature meets each year on the second Tuesday of January. The length of time the legislature meets has no limit.

Early Voting Rights

New Jersey's first constitution granted voting rights to anyone who owned land, including women and African Americans. This was an extraordinary thing. Women had few rights at this time in history, and African Americans had even fewer. In fact, most of the blacks in the **colony** were still slaves. In 1807, **legislators** amended the **constitution** and denied voting rights to all women and African Americans.

EXECUTIVE BRANCH

The executive branch of New Jersey's government carries out the state's laws. The chief executive is the governor. Voters elect the governor to a four-year **term.**

The governor is the only New Jersey executive branch official elected by the people. The governor can serve an unlimited number of terms, but not more than two in a row. New Jersey's governor appoints other people to roles in the government. This gives the governor a powerful role in forming the executive branch. The governor also works with the general assembly in forming the state's annual budget.

Other executive-branch positions include the **attorney general, secretary of state, state treasurer,** and a number of different **commissioners.** These people are all chosen by the governor, with approval from the state senate.

JUDICIAL BRANCH

New Jersey's judicial branch interprets and applies the state's laws in real-life situations. New Jersey's highest court is the state supreme court. It includes a chief justice, or judge, plus six other justices. It decides on cases covered by the constitution, and those involving **capital punishment** and other major issues. With the approval of the state senate, the governor appoints members of the supreme court to seven-year terms.

The Superior Court is the state's trial court. It also includes the **appellate** division. The governor appoints the approximately 362 members of the Superior Court to seven-year terms. They are approved by the state senate. If the governor reappoints them, they can serve until the age of 70. The appellate division of the Superior Court is made up of 32 judges who sit in 2- and 3-judge panels. They hear **appeals** from decisions of the trial courts, the tax courts, and state agencies. The kinds of courts also include **municipal** courts. The tax courts hear cases involving a person's or a business's taxes. Municipal courts are local courts. They hear basic cases involving traffic violations, less-serious crimes, and other minor violations.

The New Jersey Supreme Court hears a case involving the New Jersey Democratic Party in 2002.

New Jersey's Food

Among the many food options New Jersey offers, none is more popular than eating at a diner.

JERSEY'S DINERS

New Jersey is famous for its diners, a type of casual restaurant. Diners typically serve a wide variety of food. By some estimates, up to one-third of traditional American diners are located in New Jersey—along highways, on country roads, in small towns, and in just about every industrial area. New Jersey is sometimes called the diner **capital** of the world.

There are more diners in New Jersey than anywhere else in the world.

New Jersey's Diners

Diner culture in New Jersey is fascinating. Some regulars eat at the same place, on the same day—even in the same seat—for years! Everyone in New Jersey has his or her favorite diner. Among the most famous are:

Tick Tock Diner (Clifton)

Brooklawn Diner and Restaurant (Gloucester County)

Tops Diner (East Newark)

Olga's Diner (Marlton)

Michael's Diner & Bar (Newark)

Broadway Diner (Red Bank)

Lido Diner (Springfield)

Colonial Diner Restaurant (Woodbury)

Jerry O'Mahony is known as the creator of the Jersey Diner. He first used the word *diner* in 1913. At that time, more and more people were using automobiles. For this reason, roadside lunch wagons, where travelers could grab a quick meal, became popular. O'Mahony sold corned beef hash from horse-drawn lunch wagons in Bayonne. He noticed that the wagons looked like the dining car of a train. O'Mahony began making ready-made restaurant kits in 1913, which he called diners.

Each diner has something unique about it. For example, Olga's Diner in Marlton opened for business in 1960 and is still owned by the same family today. Some customers have been having breakfast there nearly every day for the past 30 years.

Art and Culture

New Jersey has an impressive **cultural** history. Hundreds of famous artists and entertainers were born or lived in New Jersey. Many actors and musicians sharpened their skills in the state before moving to new places. Some of these people include Frank Sinatra (1915–1998), Bruce Springsteen, and Meryl Streep.

MUSIC IN NEW JERSEY

Music lovers have many choices in the Garden State. Famous rock stars, such as Bruce Springsteen, play regularly at music clubs along the Jersey Shore.

A favorite place to hear music is the Count Basie Theater, in Red Bank, which opened in 1926. The theater is still going strong today, and stars such as Natalie Cole still perform there.

Other popular places to enjoy music in the state

Bruce Springsteen released his first album, Greetings From Asbury Park, N.J., *in 1973.*

The New Jersey Performing Arts Center (NJPAC) opened in 1997. Since that time, more than 1.6 million people have seen performances there.

include the Garden State Arts Center, in Holmdel, and the new New Jersey Performing Arts Center, in Newark.

Classical music is another popular type of entertainment in New Jersey. The New Jersey Symphony Orchestra is based in Newark. It was founded in 1846 as the Eintracht Men's Choral Society. Founded in 1919, the Plainfield Symphony Orchestra is the fourth-oldest community symphony in the United States, and Newark's Cathedral Concert Orchestra is the only professional symphony orchestra in the United States based in a cathedral.

THEATER

The theater has flourished in New Jersey for more than 100 years. Over the years, the people of New Jersey have supported stage performances, whether in a local playhouse or in a large theater. People buy more than 1.5 million tickets to musicals, dramas, and other stage performances in New Jersey each year. The McCarter Theatre, in Princeton, is a top theater that often hosts productions on their way to New York City. Critics recently named the Crossroads Theatre Company in New Brunswick as the best regional theater in the

Actors and actresses perform in a 1990s production of Camelot *at the Papermill.*

United States. The Papermill Playhouse, in Millburn, has been staging performances since 1938. The theater was created out of an old papermill that was originally built in 1795.

NEW JERSEY IN THE MOVIES

The state's mix of small towns, **industries,** seaside attractions, and **suburban** communities has made it a favorite place for filmmakers. In 2002, more than 800 television and film productions were made in New Jersey. Such recent films as *Two Weeks Notice* (2002), starring Hugh Grant and Sandra Bullock, was shot in Bayonne, Fairfield, and Jersey City. The Jennifer Lopez-Ben Affleck movie *Jersey Girl* was shot in Paulsboro, Berlin, Cherry Hill, and Highlands. In addition, many of the scenes from *Big* (1988), starring Tom Hanks, were shot in Cliffside Park.

The famous film On the Waterfront *(1954), starring Marlon Brando* (left) *and Karl Malden* (right), *was filmed in Hoboken, New Jersey.*

New Jersey's Sports

New Jersey fields professional teams in three sports. The state has also played a part in the historical roots of football, baseball, and basketball.

SPORTING FIRSTS

Football got its official start in New Jersey. In 1869, Rutgers and Princeton played the first football game in history in New Brunswick. There were 25 players on each side, and Rutgers won 6 to 4. Today, the New York Jets and Giants play their home games in East Rutherford.

In 1846, two teams played the first official game of baseball on Elysian Field in Hoboken, New Jersey. As the sport grew,

The Knickerbocker Base Ball Club of New York defeated the New York Nine 23-1 in baseball's first official game in Hoboken.

Jason Kidd of the New Jersey Nets goes up for a shot against the Los Angeles Lakers during the 2002 NBA Finals.

professional teams in New Jersey played in the National League and Federal League. In the 1930s and 1940s, Newark had the Eagles of the **Negro National League.** Baseball Hall of Famer Larry Doby (1923–2003) played for the Eagles. In 1947, Doby became the first African American to play in Major League Baseball's American League.

New Jersey was a player in the development of basketball, too. Trenton and Millville of the National Basketball League played in the first professional basketball championship in 1899. In the 1920s and 1930s, when the professional game first established its roots, more than ten New Jersey cities had their own teams. The state also had one of the greatest high-school teams in history. The Passaic High School squad, known as the Wonder Five, won 159 games in a row between 1919 and 1925. When the American Basketball Association started in 1967, the New Jersey Americans played in Teaneck. This team later became the New Jersey Nets, which reached the NBA Finals in 2002 and 2003.

THE DEVILS

New Jersey's National Hockey League (NHL) team has been one of the most successful in recent NHL history. The Devils won the NHL's Stanley Cup championship in 1995, 2000, and 2003.

Business in New Jersey

New Jersey is an important business center. Some of the world's largest corporations are headquartered there in a variety of **industries,** from communications to **pharmaceuticals.**

MAJOR NEW JERSEY COMPANIES

Among the best-known companies in New Jersey is Bell Laboratories, renamed Lucent in the 1990s. After Alexander Graham Bell (1847–1922) invented the telephone in 1876, he asked Thomas Edison to work on the receiver. This led to the formation of Bell Telephone in 1877 and American Telephone and Telegraph (AT&T) in 1885. AT&T started an engineering

Lucent, headquartered in Murray Hill, is responsible for more than 40,000 inventions since 1925.

Lucent Technologies
Bell Labs Innovations

department in 1911, then set up Bell Labs in 1925. The scientists at Bell Labs helped AT&T become one of the most successful communications companies in the world. Bell Labs has employed hundreds of thousands of New Jerseyans over the years. In 2003, Lucent employed more than 38,000 people worldwide.

Another New Jersey success story is Johnson & Johnson. It was founded in 1886 in New Brunswick by Robert Wood Johnson and his two brothers. The products the company produced had to do with the prevention of wound infections caused by airborne germs. Johnson & Johnson introduced products such as baby powder (1893), Band-Aids (1921), and Tylenol (1960). Thousands of New Jerseyans work at the Johnson & Johnson headquarters, which is still in New Brunswick.

Johnson & Johnson employs 110,300 people and sells products in more than 175 countries.

Other major retailers are located around the state. Paramus—located near several major roads and highways—became a favorite location for corporate offices. Toys R Us is based there. It is one of the largest retailers of toys, children's clothing, and baby products in the world. Easy transportation routes also attracted Bed, Bath & Beyond to Union, and Prudential Insurance to Newark.

TRANSPORTATION, CHEMICALS, AND FOOD

Other **industries** in New Jersey include transportation and shipping. In Newark, Newark

Pharmaceutical Business

New Jersey's **pharmaceutical** industries have been among the biggest employers in the state for almost 100 years. They, like other New Jersey businesses, are close to good transportation routes and a strong workforce. New Jersey's pharmaceutical companies include Hoffman-La Roche in Nutley, Merck in White House Station, Becton Dickinson in Franklin Lakes, Pfizer in Morris Plains, Schering-Plough in Kenilworth, and Wyeth in Madison.

Liberty Airport and the nearby seaport provide more than 24,000 jobs. The airport was the first one in the New York-New Jersey metropolitan area when it opened in 1928. Today, it is one of the world's busiest airports. More than 30 million passengers pass through Newark Liberty's **terminals** each year. Furthermore, the Port of New York-New Jersey is the nation's third-busiest port.

Because New Jersey lies between New York City and many states to the west and south, it is a major transportation hub. The state has the **densest** system of highways and railroads in the country. The state's more than 35,000 miles of roads include the New Jersey Turnpike, which opened in 1952. It is twelve lanes wide in some places, making it one of the widest highways in the United States.

New Jersey is also the largest chemical-producing state in the nation. For example, DuPont has a factory in Parlin that makes Teflon and other nonstick coatings, as well as inkjet color proofing systems for color printers. Dow Chemical also has several sites in the state.

Campus Crowd

Education is another type of business in New Jersey. Two of the state's universities, Princeton (1746) and Rutgers (1766), have a long history. They both started before the **American Revolution.** In 1869, they played each other in the first football game in history. Two U.S. presidents—James Madison and

Woodrow Wilson—and more than 80 U.S. senators went to Princeton. Rutgers has three campuses today, in New Brunswick, Newark, and Camden. Historians think that the word *campus* was first used to describe the setting of Princeton.

Food production has always been important in New Jersey. For example, Campbell Soup Company began in Camden and is still a major employer in the city. Seabrook Farms, the first company to quick-freeze fruits and vegetables in the 1930s, is in Seabrook.

The Campbell Soup Company started in 1869 as the Joseph A. Campbell Preserve Company.

Legends and Lore

Some of New Jersey's legends involve the pirates who hid in the many **inlets** along the Atlantic coast during the 1600s and 1700s. Some stories are truthful, while others are either difficult to prove or just plain hard to believe.

CAPTAIN KIDD

One pirate story involves the famous Captain Kidd, or William Kidd (1645–1701), as he was known when he lived in New Jersey. In 1695, the British asked William Kidd, who was a sea captain, to attack French ships off the Atlantic coast. Kidd could keep whatever he took, and the British would scare the French away. Captain Kidd soon had a small fortune. He started investing in taverns, docks, and whaling ships from Cape May north to Massachusetts.

Kidd became fearless, and in 1697 he attacked an English ship from India called the *Quedagh Merchant*. Captain Kidd then fled to New York in search of safety. However, he was turned over to the English, who hanged him in 1701. The legend says that before Captain Kidd docked in New

Captain Kidd may have buried his treasure on the Jersey Shore.

Bartholomew Roberts, born in Wales, sank more than 400 ships.

Calico Jack always wore an outfit made from calico, a type of cotton that was made in Calcutta, India.

York, he buried much of his treasure in the sands of the New Jersey coast. Historians say it is worth millions of dollars and perhaps a great deal more. Yet, after more than 300 years, no one has ever found any of it.

BARTHOLOMEW ROBERTS

A few years after Captain Kidd was hanged, Bartholomew Roberts (1682–1722) began attacking ships. Every seafaring country wanted to punish him, and he moved his ships to the mid-Atlantic coast. A storm then blew him north to Cape May in the spring of 1720.

The locals recognized Roberts's ships and attempted to capture him. They stopped him in Delaware Bay, but he was able to escape. New Jersey **colonists** sank one of his vessels in the battle, sending a boatload of gold and silver to the bottom. No one has ever been able to find the wreck and claim the fortune.

CALICO JACK

Another New Jersey story involved two women—Mary Read and Ann Bonny. Mary Read lived with her mother until she was thirteen years old, and then she worked as a servant. She dressed like a man and joined the British army. Later, Read joined the crew of a British warship. The pirate Calico Jack Rackham captured the ship, and he began killing his prisoners. Read revealed her true identity, and the pirate decided not to kill her.

Life Savers

Not all legendary figures from the Atlantic coast were criminals. Some of them were heroes who saved many lives. At one time, 50 to 100 ships a year sank off the New Jersey coast. Most were pushed into shallow water by storms, where they broke up and sank on the shifting sandbars. In the 1800s, rescue teams used special cannons to shoot ropes to the boats, and passengers would travel to shore inside special containers pulled by rescue crews. Eventually, New Jersey built lifesaving stations every 3.5 miles from Sandy Hook to the southern tip of Long Beach Island.

From this system grew the U.S. Lifesaving Service, which quickly expanded to cover the entire Atlantic coast, the shores of the Great Lakes, the beaches on the Gulf of Mexico, and the coast of the Pacific Ocean.

Sailing with Calico Jack, Read became friends with Bonny, the pirate's wife. He grew jealous of this friendship and put Read ashore in Cape May, where she bought some land and opened a store. The pirate continued to steal from boats off Long Island and New Jersey. He used Read's store to hide the loot he stole. When local authorities figured out what was going on, they burned the store. British ships surrounded Calico Jack in Delaware Bay and forced him to surrender.

The British put Rackham, Bonny, and Read on trial in England, and they were found guilty of piracy. They hanged Calico Jack in 1720 but decided not to hang the two women. Read died in prison after the trial, but records indicate that Bonny simply disappeared. Some people believe that her father, a lawyer living in the **colonies,** helped her change her name. They say that she returned to Ocean City, New Jersey, where she lived out her life as Mary Pritchard. Pritchard never admitted that she was Ann Bonny, but when Pritchard died, among her belongings were things that belonged to Bonny's father. No one has ever solved this mystery.

The New Jersey Devil

No discussion of New Jersey lore would be complete without talking about the New Jersey Devil. Hundreds of people claim to have seen it. Most think that it lives in the remote Pine Barrens, in the southern part of the state. Although no one has ever captured, killed, or photographed it, there is a sketch of the devil. It looks like a serpent with the head of a horse, wings of a bird, and claws of a dinosaur.

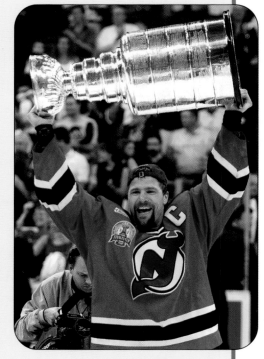

During the 1700s and 1800s, the New Jersey Devil was little more than a local story. But in 1909, so many people saw it that it became national news. After appearances in the 1950s and 1960s, the devil faded from the headlines and was mostly forgotten. In 1982, when the Colorado Rockies of the National Hockey League moved to the Meadowlands Sports Complex, in East Rutherford, the devil was back in the news. After considering many different names, the team decided to call itself the New Jersey Devils.

TRAGEDIES

New Jersey was the scene of two world-famous events—the kidnapping of Charles Lindbergh Jr. and the *Hindenburg* air tragedy.

Lindbergh was famous for flying the Spirit of St. Louis *all by himself from New York City to Paris, France, in 33 hours and 30 minutes on May 20–21, 1927.*

Aviator Charles Lindbergh (1902–1974), the first man to complete a **solo** flight across the Atlantic Ocean, was a celebrity who liked his privacy. He and his wife and son lived in the quiet town of Hopewell during the early 1930s. On March 1, 1932, someone took twenty-month-old Charles Jr. from his bedroom. The Lindberghs received a note demanding a $50,000 **ransom** payment. They paid the kidnappers, but the people did not return their son. Later, Charles Jr. was found dead. Bruno Hauptman, a criminal who was in the country illegally, was accused of the crime. Hauptman claimed he was innocent throughout the trial, but he was found guilty by the court. In 1935, the Lindberghs left the United States to live in England.

In May 1937, the landing of the luxury airship *Hindenburg* attracted a crowd of reporters to the New Jersey shore town of Lakehurst. It was completing a flight from Germany and was docking in New Jersey. The transatlantic flight took two days and cost $400 per person—which would be about $5,000 in today's money. As the ship neared the ground, it burst into flames. The fire burned out so fast that, of the 97 people aboard, only 36 died.

The *Hindenburg,* built in Germany, is still the largest airship that was ever flown. At a length of more than 800 feet, it was more than 4 times the size of today's 192-foot-long Goodyear blimps. The *Hindenburg* would also dwarf Boeing's 231-foot-long 747 jumbo jet.

The Hindenburg's *hydrogen gas ignited, leading to an explosion. Today's blimps use helium, which will not burn.*

Attractions and Landmarks

From the Jersey Shore to Newark, New Jersey has activities and attractions for people of all ages.

JERSEY SHORE

The Jersey Shore is the state's most popular vacation spot. It stretches for 130 miles, from the tip of Sandy Hook south past Atlantic City along the coast of the Atlantic Ocean. There are many **boardwalks** along this stretch of coast, many of which were built in the late 1800s and early 1900s. The boardwalks offer scenic strolls, beach access, and countless shops, restaurants, and other amusements.

Some boardwalks, such as the one at Asbury Park, have faded away. Others are busy year-

More than 32 million people visit the Atlantic City Boardwalk each year.

Millions of people enjoy New Jersey's beaches, such as this one in Atlantic City.

round. The five-mile stretch of boardwalk in Atlantic City, for example, is filled with tourists even in poor weather. The city first built the boardwalk as a temporary structure in 1870, and it proved immensely popular. It was the first boardwalk in the world. An 1889 hurricane destroyed the old boardwalk, and it was replaced with a sturdy, 60-foot-wide version with several **piers.** This is the boardwalk in use today.

A popular **promenade** along the Atlantic coast stretches for several miles from Weehawken to North Bergen, in Hudson County. Built atop the cliffs of the Palisades, it runs along Boulevard East and overlooks the Hudson River and the New York skyline. The view of the sunrise over New York's skyscrapers each morning and the reflected light off these buildings each evening at sunset are equally spectacular.

NATURAL WONDERS

New Jersey is filled with a wide variety of natural wonders. For example, the 500-foot high Palisades cliffs tower above the Hudson River. Formed four million years ago, they played an important role in the early days of filmmaking, in the early 1900s. When filmmakers produced silent films in New York and New

New Jersey State Parks

Delaware National Scenic River
High Point
Delaware River
Wawayanda
Swartswood
Long Pond Ironworks
Ringwood
Ramapo Mountain
Kittatinny Valley
Norvin Green
Lake Hopatcong
Hopatcong
Farny
Paramus
Allamuchy / Stephens
Paterson
Jenny Jump
Passaic
Fort Lee
Hacklebarney
Livingston
S. Branch Raritan River
N. Branch Raritan River
Newark
Hoboken
Jersey City
Voorhees
Washington Rock
Bayonne
Liberty
Spruce Run Rec Area
Round Valley Rec Area
Perth Amboy
Bull's Island Rec Area
New Brunswick
Cheesequake
Leonardo Marina
Princeton
Princeton Battlefield
Washington Crossing
Ewing
Long Branch
Monmouth Battlefield
Trenton
Neptune
Allaire
Toms River
Willingboro
Rancocas
ATLANTIC OCEAN
Camden
Cherry Hill
Browns Mills
Haddonfield
Double Trouble
Forked River Marina
Island Beach
Barngat Lighthouse
Delaware River
Penn
Ft. Mott
Pine Barrons
N
W E
S
Parvin
Vineland
Farley Marina
Atlantic City
0   20 mi.
Corson's Inlet
▲ State Park
Villas
Cape May Point
Cape May

Jersey, the Palisades were a favorite shooting location. In fact, the term *cliff-hanger* comes from *Perils of Pauline*—a film that featured several daring stunts performed on the cliffs of Fort Lee, which overlooks the Hudson River and the Manhattan skyline.

In Sandy Hook—which has two million visitors each year—is North America's only remaining natural **holly** forest. Most visitors do not even realize it is there. Across the Sandy Hook bay is Monmouth Hills, a unique, wooded area that is one of the state's oldest **planned communities**—and one of the highest points on the East Coast. Author James Fenimore Cooper

A Famous Duel

Aaron Burr (1756–1836) and Alexander Hamilton (1755 or 1757–1804) were two political rivals who lived during the late 1700s and early 1800s. At dawn on the morning of July 11, 1804, their hatred for each other led to a famous **duel** on the cliffs at Weehawken. Both men took ten paces, turned, and fired. Hamilton fell and died the following day.

(1789–1851) called it "the most beautiful combination of land and water in America" when he visited the area in the 1830s.

The Great Falls of the Passaic River are in Paterson. The falls mark the spot where the river tumbles over the first ridge of the Watchung Mountains. In the days before tourists discovered Niagara Falls, near Buffalo, New York, Paterson's falls were one of the most-visited natural wonders in the United States. This sight has been the subject of countless paintings and prints. It is famous not just for its 77-foot drop, but because it is close to one of the state's most **industrialized** areas. The town of Paterson was built at the base of the falls in the 1790s so that the great amount of rushing water could power its factories.

New Jersey has several other unique natural areas, including the Pine Barrens in the southern part of the state. The Pine Barrens covers nearly 2,000 square miles between Cape May and southern Monmouth County. It has more wilderness and open space than any other place on the mid-Atlantic

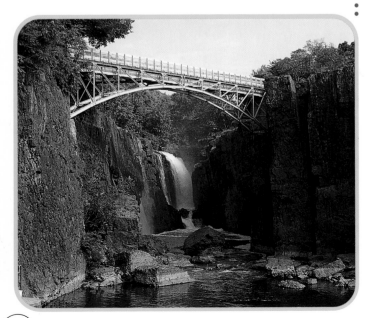

The Great Falls of the Passaic River are the second highest falls in the eastern United States.

Lucy the Elephant

One of the oddest attractions on the Jersey Shore is Lucy, the Margate elephant. Lucy is 6 stories tall and weighs 90 tons. James Lafferty built Lucy in 1881 to promote the sale of seaside properties he owned. Lafferty also built huge elephants for Coney Island and Cape May, but Lucy is the only one still standing.

coast. It was the first national reserve in the nation. The United Nations classifies the Pine Barrens as a biosphere reserve. This means that it is an example of one of the world's major types of **ecosystems.**

New Jersey's Great Swamp is not as well known as the Pine Barrens, but it still has more than 350,000 visitors a year. Like the Pine Barrens, the Great Swamp is home to hundreds of kinds of plant and animal **species.** Located south of Morristown, this low-lying area covers 7,454 acres

The Pine Barrens is the largest area of open space on the mid-Atlantic seaboard between Richmond, Virginia, and Boston, Massachusetts.

Rock and Roll Central

Asbury Park was once a popular seaside **resort.** In the 1970s and 1980s, its popularity as a resort declined. But people started visiting Asbury Park for its music. Bruce Springsteen was the first nationally known musician to come from the music clubs of Asbury Park. Many other talented musicians also played there.

and has some of the few remaining trees that date back to the time before Europeans arrived. To preserve the Great Swamp's natural state, laws prohibit human-made structures and vehicles from entering most of the park.

To the north of the Great Swamp are lakes Hopatcong, Musconetcong, and Marshipacong. Located in the rolling forests of northern New Jersey, they have unusual shapes. Hopatcong is the state's largest lake. It has more than 30 **inlets** along its 41-mile shoreline, as well as 3 major islands.

The Great Swamp was designated a national wildlife refuge in 1968. More than 350,000 people visit it each year.

Farther north are the Delaware Water Gap and Skylands regions. Canoers, campers, and hikers explore the wilderness of the Delaware Water Gap. The Delaware River created the Delaware Water Gap as it cut through the Kittatinny Mountains. The oldest rocks in New Jersey form the Skylands, in the northwest corner of the state.

MUSEUMS

Museums are another popular attraction in New Jersey. The State Museum in Trenton opened in 1895 with a small exhibit of rocks. Today, it has all kinds of collections, such as dinosaur **fossils,** fine art, and Native American **artifacts.** The Liberty Science Center, in nearby Jersey City, is known for its hands-on exhibits. And the Edison Tower and Museum can be found in Menlo Park. Among the state's many popular small museums is the Yogi Berra Museum in Montclair.

The Thomas A. Edison Memorial Tower and Menlo Park Museum was built in 1937, and is located on the exact spot where Edison had his laboratory. Edison's Kinetoscope was the first device to record and reproduce objects in motion.

New Jersey's Bridges and Structures

New Jersey's noteworthy structures include bridges, tunnels, and several famous lighthouses

BRIDGES

With water surrounding the state on three sides—and countless rivers and **inlets** cutting into and through it—it is no surprise to learn that New Jersey has more than 6,000 bridges. Its most famous is the George Washington Bridge (GWB), which opened on October 25, 1931. It spans 4,760 feet across the Hudson River between Fort Lee, New Jersey, and New York City. The GWB has two levels. The lower level was opened in 1962. This made

The American Institute for Steel Construction named the Bayonne Bridge as the most beautiful steel arch bridge of 1931.

the GWB the world's only fourteen-lane suspension bridge, and it is currently one of the world's busiest bridges. In 2002, nearly 58 million cars passed over the bridge. The GWB also flies the largest free-flying American flag in the world. Its stripes are about five feet wide, and its stars are about four feet in diameter.

The Bayonne Bridge links Bayonne with Staten Island. It, too, was completed in 1931. It has steel arches. The Benjamin Franklin Bridge, which spans the Delaware River between New Jersey and Pennsylvania, was the longest suspension bridge in the world when it opened in 1926. Another of New Jersey's best-known bridges is the Pulaski Skyway, which stretches more than three miles across the Passaic and Hackensack rivers just east of Newark. When finished in 1932, it was the state's first elevated highway.

The George Washington Bridge's towers rise 604 feet above the water.

New Jersey's bridges include many old drawbridges, mostly across rivers and inlets near the Atlantic coast. The amount of traffic in these areas has increased in recent years due to the growing population, and some people find the bridges to be an inconvenience. The state may replace them with taller, permanent bridges, as it did its covered bridges, which were also an inconvenience to motorists. Today, only one of these

Fields of Honor

During the **American Revolution,** the **colonists** and the British fought more than 100 battles on New Jersey soil. State parks, historical sites, and museums mark some of the spots where these battles took place. The most famous sites are in Trenton, Freehold, and Morristown. In Trenton, George Washington defeated the **hessians** in 1776. In Freehold, the Continental Army first proved it could stand up to the British on a traditional battlefield. In Morristown, Washington's troops survived one of the most brutal New Jersey winters on record.

wooden structures remains: Green Sergeants' covered bridge. It is more than 150 years old and is located in Sergeantsville.

TUNNELS

Not all traffic in New Jersey moves over the water. The Holland Tunnel connects Jersey City with lower Manhattan. Completed in 1927, people called it the Eighth Wonder of the World for many years. One of the biggest challenges for building the tunnel was ventilation, or fresh air, for the people passing through the tunnel.

Cars enter the Holland Tunnel, which was built underneath the Hudson River.

Engineers thought that poisonous automobile exhaust fumes would make travel through the tunnel impossible. However, they designed an automatic ventilation system that produced purer air in the tunnel than was found outside! Fresh air is supplied to the tunnel every 90 seconds. The air is moved by 42 blowing and 42 exhaust fans arranged in 4 ventilation buildings. Nearly sixteen million cars passed through the Holland Tunnel in 2002.

A few miles north, the Lincoln Tunnel runs underneath the Hudson River from the foot of the Palisades in Weehawken to midtown Manhattan. It opened in 1937. Nearly 21 million people passed through the Lincoln Tunnel in 2002.

LIGHTHOUSES

New Jersey's coastline runs for more than 130 miles and has many lighthouses. Thirty-four historic lighthouses dot the New Jersey coast. The **octagon**-shaped Sandy Hook lighthouse played a big role for the British during the American Revolution. It served as a beacon for ships sailing in and out of New York Harbor. It was the spot from which troops were sent to Philadelphia and New York. Perhaps the most amazing thing about the Sandy Hook lighthouse is that it is still there. On several occasions **colonists** attempted to blow it up, but it survived every

Sandy Hook lighthouse opened in 1764.

The Barnegat Lighthouse is visible for twenty miles out to sea.

attack. Today, the U.S. Coast Guard takes care of the Sandy Hook lighthouse, which is the oldest continually working lighthouse in the United States.

Across the **channel** from Sandy Hook, two light towers date to the 1850s. One is on the water in Leonardo. The other is on Beacon Hill in Middletown. For many years, these lights helped sailors find their way to Sandy Hook Bay. A few miles south of them, at the mouth of the Navesink River, are the famous Twin Lights in Highlands. A close look reveals that these lighthouses are not twins at all—one is round, the other **octagonal.** In 1899, the Italian scientist Guglielmo Marconi selected this spot for the first demonstration of his wireless telegraph.

New Jersey's most famous lighthouse is the Barnegat Lighthouse, in Barnegat. Nicknamed "Old Barney," it is one of the most-visited, most-painted, and most-photographed lighthouses in the world. George Meade, who became a general in the **Civil War** (1861–1865), designed and built the Barnegat Lighthouse in 1859. It was in service until 1927. New Jersey later used it during World War II (1939–1945) to search for German submarines, which attacked several ships off the New Jersey coast.

Map of New Jersey

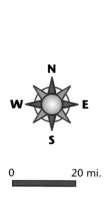

N
W E
S

0   20 mi.

New York

Pennsylvania

New Jersey

Atlantic
Ocean

Delaware

Delaware River

Lake
Hopatcong

S. Branch Raritan River

N. Branch Raritan River

Mahwah

Passaic
Hackensack

Wayne
Paterson

Paramus
Teaneck
Fort Lee

West Orange
Livingston

North Bergen
Hoboken
Jersey City

Morristown
Newark

Elizabeth
Bayonne

Piscataway
Plainfield

Edison

Perth Amboy

New Brunswick

Sandy Hook

Matawan
Holmdel

Red Bank

Princeton

Long Branch

Ewing

Trenton

Asbury Park

Toms River

Willingboro

Browns Mills

Lakehurst
Point Pleasant

Camden

Cherry Hill
Haddonfield
Marlton

Delaware River

Barnegat

Long Beach
Island

Vineland

Millville

ATLANTIC
OCEAN

Atlantic City

Ocean City

Avalon

Villas

Cape May

Glossary

artifact object made by humans, such as a tool, pottery, or a weapon

American Revolution American fight for independence from British rule between 1775 and 1783

appeal ask that a case be taken to a higher court to be heard again

appellate a court that reviews decisions made by lower courts

attorney general chief law officer of a nation or state

aviator the operator or pilot of an aircraft, especially an airplane

boardwalk wide sidewalk, usually made of boards, located near the water at a shore

capital location of a government

capital punishment death penalty for a crime

capitol building in which the legislature meets

census official count of the number of people in a place

channel body of water joining two larger bodies of water

Civil War the war between the Northern and Southern states of the United States from 1861 to 1865.

commissioner official who is the head of a government department

constitution plan for government

cornucopia a horn-shaped container

culture ideas, skills, arts, and way of life of a certain people at a certain time

dense crowded together

duel combat between two persons fought with deadly weapons and with witnesses present

economy use or management of money

ecosystem community of living things, together with the environment in which they live

fossil the remains of an ancient plant or animal. Most fossils are remains that have turned to stone or whose outlines have been preserved in stone.

general assembly one of the houses of a state legislature

hessian German soldier serving in the British army during the American Revolution

holly tree with spiny evergreen leaves and sometimes red berries, whose branches are often used for Christmas decorations

industry group of businesses that offer a similar product or service

inlet small or narrow bay

legislature governmental body that makes and changes laws. A legislator is a lawmaker.

marl loose, crumbly soil usually made of clay, sand, and calcium carbonate. It is used in making cement and as a fertilizer.

memorial helping to remember some person, thing, or event

municipal having to do with a city or town

Negro National League a baseball league for African Americans. African Americans were not allowed to play in Major League Baseball until the late 1940s.

octagon eight-sided shape

pharmaceutical having to do with medicine

pier structure built out into the water to use as a place for ships or boats to land or for people to walk

piping trimming stitched in the seams or along the edges of clothing

planned community living area designed around a master plan for buildings, homes, and businesses

promenade place for walking

ransom price demanded before a captured person is set free

resort place for recreation

rotunda a round room with a high ceiling

secretary of state official responsible for keeping state records

solo by oneself

species a certain related group of animals

state treasurer person in charge of the money of a state government

suburb city or town just outside a larger city. Suburban means having to do with a suburb

term set period of time

terminal passenger station located at the end of a transportation line

urban relating to the city

More Books to Read

Boraas, Tracy. *New Jersey.* Minnetonka, Minn.: Capstone Press, 2003.

Holtz, Eric Siegfried. *New Jersey: The Garden State.* Milwaukee: Gareth Stevens, 2002.

Nault, Jennifer. *A Guide to New Jersey.* New York City: Weigl Publishers, Inc., 2001.

Scholl, Elisabeth. *New Jersey.* Danbury, Conn.: Scholastic Library Publishing, 2002.

Stewart, Mark. *New Jersey History.* Chicago: Heinemann Library, 2003.

Index

American Revolution 4–5, 34
appellate courts 15
art and culture 18–20
Asbury Park 18, 33, 38
Atlantic city boardwalk 33–34
attractions and landmarks 33–39
  Asbury Park 18, 33, 38
  Great Falls of the Passaic River 36
  Great Swamp 37–38
  Jersey Shore 33–34
  Palisades cliffs 34–36
  Pine Barrens 36–37
  Sandy Hook 35–36

Barnegat Lighthouse 44
Bayonne Bridge 41
boardwalks 33–34
bridges 40–42
businesses 23–26

capital 11
capitol 11–12
constitution 12, 14
courts 14–15

diners 16–17

facts about New Jersey 4
food 16–17

George Washington Bridge 40–41
government 11–15
  executive branch 14
  judicial branch 14–15
  legislative branch 12–14
Great Falls of the Passaic River 36

Great Swamp 37–38
Hindenburg, crash of 32
Holland Tunnel 42–43

inventors 5

Jersey Shore 33–34
Johnson & Johnson 24

legends 27–30
lighthouses 43–44
Lincoln Tunnel 43
Lindbergh, Charles 31
Lucent (Bell Laboratories) 23–24
Lucy, the Margate elephant 37

movies 20
municipal courts 15
museums 39
music 18–19

New Jersey Devil 30
New Jersey legislature 12–14
New Jersey Performing Arts Center 19

Palisades cliffs 34–36
Pine Barrens 36–37

Sandy Hook 35, 36, 44
Sandy Hook lighthouse 43–44
sports 21–22
  baseball 21–22
  basketball 22
  basketball, high school 22
  football 21
  hockey 22
Springsteen Bruce 18

state government 16–22
  capitol 11–12
  legislative branch 12–13
  executive branch 14
  judicial branch 14–15
state symbols 6–10
  bird 7
  dinosaur 9
  flag 6
  flower 8
  nickname 9
  quarter 10
  seal 7
  shell 8–9
  song (unofficial) 10
  trees 8
Superior Court 15
Supreme Court of New Jersey 14, 15
symphony orchestras 19

Tax Court 15
theaters 19–20
Thomas A. Edison Memorial Tower and Menlo Park Museum 39
transportation 24–25
Trenton 11
tunnels 42–43

About the Author

Mark Stewart makes his home in New Jersey. A graduate of Duke University with a degree in history, Stewart has authored more than 100 nonfiction titles for the school and library market. He and his wife Sarah have two daughters, Mariah and Rachel.